I0200911

gondolin press

Emanuele and Francesco Sartori

MYSTIC DANCE

A poem on the Resurrection

parallel italian/english translation

gondolin press

MYSTIC DANCE – Emanuele and Francesco Sartori

Original title: *Mistica danza* (2017)
© Fede & Cultura (Italy)
www.fedecultura.com
Translator: Peter Waymel

© gondolin press
1331 Red Cedar Cir
80524 Fort Collins CO

www.gondolinpress.com
info@gondolinpress.com

2018 © Gondolin Institute LLC
Book ISBN 978-1-945658-10-5

All the literary and artistic rights are reserved. The rights for trans-la-tion, electronic storage, copy and total or partial adaptation, by any equipment, (including microfilm and photostats) are reserved for all countries. The publisher is at any of the untraceable entitles disposal.

First Italian edition: June 2017

First U.S. edition: April 2019

PREFACE

I was an atheist, or better said, an anti-theist. I hated God and especially the Catholic Church. I lived in a state of intellectual agnosticism, existential atheism, familial, socio-political and moral rebellion, with an active anti-Christian militancy begun in the Marxist-Leninist movements and developed in those of an anarchic-radical stamp until I reached and embraced philosophical and existential Nihilism. All this was leading me to the darkness of spiritual despair, serious psychic depression, various forms of addiction and dabbling in the occult.

Yet I continued in my pride and in the neopositivist presumption that man was enough for himself and that science and technology would free us from death, pain and the fatigue of living. Aestheticizing hedonism was my existential timbre... Add whatever you can imagine that would follow on a practical and daily level, and you will have drawn a man who attempted to overcome the human, as my wicked masters had hoped: Marx, Freud, Nietzsche, Sartre, Camus, the Frankfurt School, just to name a few.

Only one woman, a classmate, continued to love me since high school and loved me for roughly ten years, though suffering my trantrums and my limitless selfishness. I did not understand how it was possible to love the opposite of that which one hopes and believes. Then she yielded to the obstinacy of my delusions of grandeur and rightly shaped for herself a different life. Now I thank her publicly for having loved me so intensely, giving me all of herself without expecting anything in return and helping me avoid an untimely end. I humbly ask her forgiveness for what she suffered because of me, just as I ask forgiveness from the other people that I may have offended with my behavior.

Thinking back on it, however, a posteriori I can affirm with certainty that she was the sign of how another Woman clearly drew close to me, immediately after the end of the preceding relationship, with discretion and, always leaving me free, shone a different Light in my eyes, helping me slowly change course to show me the Source of this Light, which was given to me gratuitously, in the divine *Agàpe* incarnate in daily life. My conversion was a difficult one and passed through crises that bordered on suicide.

But it was an authentic *metànoia*. Now, thanks to particular interior illuminations, which I repute to be supernatural, and the help of Fathers in the Faith, such as Servant of God Fr. Leone (see the *Introduction* and *note 3*). I threw away various addictions, seasoned with pharmaceuticals, psychiatrists and psychoanalysts of all schools, with the false teachers in philosophy and literature (*the avantgardes, the accursed poets...*).

I found myself dialoguing with only one person, Jesus. And with his mother, Mary. To the *modern* reader all this will seem to be the proof of my folly. But it is not. In fact, the last step (very painful on they psycho-physical and spiritual level) that separated me from the Door of Light consisted in being liberated, by exorcism, of a real personal and negative presence that intended to annihilate me, which had bound me at a young age through a curse; I became aware of this thanks to my mother's memories and private revelations made under exorcism.

The Prince of Darkness did not want to let me go towards the Love of the Father. But *Love is stronger than death...* (cf. *Sgs* 8:6-7). And the Father was keeping for me an *Amour* (understood as *agàpe*: oblative, gratuitous love, which does not ask for or expect anything in return): on December 8, 1986, Solemnity of the *Immaculate Conception*, he made me find, apparently by chance (now we say *providentially*), seated at my side during the Holy Mass, the stupendous person who would become my wife: I touched her physically for the first time, on that very occasion, during the liturgical *Kiss of Peace*. Thanks to her, God has given us three wonderful children and even more, has shown us that a true marriage is kept safe in the hands of the great Helmsman: Jesus. In good weather and in storms He has always helped us be reborn with reciprocal forgiveness in the purifying fire of the Love that comes from God: the Spirit of Jesus hovers over our lives and heals past wounds, orienting us ever more in the desire to live in Him, with Him, for Him.

All this merits a separate treatment, but in any event: here you have the poetic version of the tale (already presented in my preceding book[1]), while perhaps in the near future another book will address the story in another literary form and with new and dramatic angles.

My son Emanuele, born in 1994, at sixteen wanted to find the source of happiness in life, but took one wrong turn after another. He, too, was the victim of a curse, orchestrated out of hatred of the Faith of our whole family, by members of a powerful secret organization that venerates Lucifer/Satan as the *true good god* (*sic!*).

But for Emanuele, too, the Mother of God crushed the head of the *serpent!* His poems were, in fact, inspired after a sudden conversion to the Catholic faith, which took place January 1, 2012, entirely out of grace given from on High, while he was living a disordered and deviant life, but one always marked by the desire for truth and happiness.

Simultaneous to his conversion marked by a General confession, the Holy Mass of the Epiphany and having received the Holy Eucharist, phenomena began to occur of a clearly demoniacal nature: blasphemous obsessions, bodily disturbances and sudden aversions to the sacred, physical and psychic blockages, horrifying sensory hallucinations... But his poems bespeak the mystic spirit that pervades him now, after four years of infinite tears and sufferings caused by believing himself to be abandoned by God. The verses flowed spontaneously and rapidly, almost unconsciously, a month after Emanuele had prayed to God the Father for the ability to write poems in honor of the Blessed Virgin Mary.

It was at Lourdes, however, at the end of May 2016, following an exorcism in a semitic language (likely in Aramaic) done by a qualified priest who was an ex-missionary in the Middle East and Africa, that he had the Grace to see before him the way for his liberation from the bonds of the Evil One. The confessor-exorcist directed him without hesitation to the *Association of Our Lady of Lourdes - St. Luigi Orione* with headquarters in Missaglia (Lecco, Italy), where Pino and various volunteers work to alleviate the sufferings of those sick in the body, mind and above all spirit, through powerful prayers of Liberation and Healing, able to cast out demons from souls obsessed, vexed and possessed, especially if they are victims of curses and spells perpetrated by satanic sects, etc.

At Lourdes, after the bath in the pool I, instead, was pervaded by an unspeakable joy and peace and I entrusted myself to the Sacred Hearts of Jesus, Mary and St. Joseph. Since then our life has changed radically. In the sense that we know Whom we must love and whom we must fight inside ourselves and out, with the weapons that God gives us to win every time the tempter draws near: the Holy Mass with the Holy Eucharist, daily if possible, periodical sacramental Confession, Eucharistic Adoration, the Holy Rosary, meditation on the Word of God, continual Prayer, which means, besides reciting with the heart frequent ejaculatory prayers, keeping our mind, our affectivity, our will undivided and directed towards the Father of all Mercy, who wants our happiness both on earth, though amid sufferings and persecutions, and above in the Kingdom of Heaven for eternity.

Now we fear nothing. God alone is enough for us.

«Nada te turbe
nada te espante,
todo se pasa,
Dios no se muda;
la paciencia
todo lo alcanza;

quien a Dios tiene
nada le falta.
Solo Dios basta».[2]

May this rather uncommon experience of ours encourage everyone to abandon the false modern myths of progress in a single direction (economic materialism, hedonism and biological reductionism), ethical and ontological self-sufficiency (horizontal humanism, emotive pan-sexualism, *gender fluidity*), the practical exclusion of God from everyday life (atheism and immorality, almost consequences of believing and of making of man a god). Of course, if we want, man is a god, but a *god of trash!* A slave of his true adversary, Satan, who whispers in our ears that with him we will be free, happy, satisfied in all the desires and pleasures of this world. But soon we will discover that his gifts are the trap, the seduction to make us his slaves forever in the kingdom of darkness, in the kingdom of the Prince of Lies and a Murderer from the start (cf *John* 8:44), in his eternal kingdom and with no escape, after we have made a definitive rejection, perhaps coinciding with our last breath, of the umpteenth and extreme invitation to welcome the Love of God expressed in Jesus, the Eternal and Incarnate *Lògos*, repenting of the evil we have freely chosen and intentionally carried out in our life.

Francesco Sartori

Summary

Mystic dance

Francesco Sartori

Poesie di Francesco Sartori

«La santità consiste... non tanto nell'amare Dio,
quanto nel lasciarsi amare da Lui,
o piuttosto consiste nell'amare
lasciandosi amare da Lui,
accettando il Suo amore,
perché accettare di essere amati
significa amare, significa dare».

Servo di Dio Padre LEONE HABERSTROH
della Società del Verbo Divino
(nato in terra a Mariazell - Germania - 24/07/1905;
nato in Cielo da Padova - 08/01/1986)

Poems by Francesco Sartori

«Holiness consists... not so much in loving God,
as in letting oneself be loved by Him,
or rather it consists in loving
by letting oneself be loved by Him,
accepting His love,
because to accept to be loved
means to love, it means to give».

Servant of God Fr. LEO HABERSTROH [3]

of the Society of the Divine Word
(born on earth in Mariazell - Germany - 7/24/1905;
born in Heaven from Padua - 1/8/1986).

Il ripostiglio
ove le tue angosce
s'acquetano
a volte
riverbera di luce
all'imbrunire.

Piano m'appresso a leggere
tra le fessure delle porte,
da te così ben serrate,
quale richiamo avranno
questi giorni incerti
in cui sperare è contro ragione
e ragionare è contro esistere.
Ma io continuo a cercare
ove riposano le parole
ritagliate
nel quotidiano incedere del tempo
e presto disperse nel vento…

Lassù
sulla montagna
tra le nebbie alpine
appena scalfite

Reverberations of love

The closet
where your anxieties
are allayed
sometimes
reverberates with light
at dusk.

Slowly I draw near to read
between the cracks of the doors,
so tightly closed by you,
what echo
these uncertain days will have
in which hope goes against reason and reason
goes against existing.
But I continue to search
for the resting place of words
cut out
in the daily passing of time
and soon dispersed in the wind...

Up there
on the mountain
among the alpine mists
lightly touched

dal verso dell'ùpupa.

O laggiù,

in tuoni e languori,

in nere visïoni

e illuminati sogni,

nei precisi intagli

d'incubati incagli.

Sei lì

ad attendermi fedele.

Unisoni

    a vegliare

        l'impalpabile cuore

            esplodere

                danzando

        nel cristallino

      canto

    della sera.

E la prima parola

        si liquefa

           in chiaroscuri

                riverberi d'amore.

          E bagliori

        s'incuneano

      in spiragli di dolori

    a inventarsi

antichi ardori.

by the call of the hoopoe.
Or down there,
in thunder and languor,
in black visions
and bright dreams,
in the precise carvings
of incubated things run to ground.
You are there
waiting for me, faithful.
In unison
      keeping vigil
            over the impalpable heart
                  which explodes
                        dancing
                in the crystalline
           song
     of evening.
And the first word
           liquefies
               in light and dark
                   reverberations of love.
             And flashes
          wedge themselves
       into spirals of pain,
    inventing
ancient ardors.

Allora
la tua voce
ritempra
la china,
sbalza
gli occhi,
rimpalla
le arterie,
richiama
d'incanto
la brezza
del tuo
primo
svestito
rossore...

    ...destino
        schiarito
            e subito
                nell'aere
                    rapito.

Then
your voice
fortifies
the descent,
bounces
to the eyes,
rebounds
off the arteries,
recalls
enchanted
the breeze
of your
first
undressed
redness...

        ...destiny

            made clear

                and immediately

                    into the heavens

                        taken up.

Nel bosco di faggi e querce
ho rincorso una voce
che chiamava
lontana
lassù dalla montagna.

La sterpaglia
frenava i miei piedi
ed io attorcigliavo le mani
tra rami secchi e muti.

Grondava sangue
la cima del faggio
e la quercia dimenava
i suoi rami strillanti.

Al cielo
il mio sguardo
non vedeva che ombre,
fantasmi di *ferryboats*,
ove cagliavano
ridicole idee
d'onnipotenza vacua.

In the forest of beech and oak
I chased a voice
that called
far away
up there from the mountain.

The brush
curbed my feet
and I twisted my hands
amid dry and silent branches.

The top of the beech
was dripping blood
and the oak wiggled
its screaming branches.

In the sky,
my eyes
could only see shadows,
ghosts of ferryboats,
where ridiculous ideas
of empty omnipotence
swirled.

«Grida più forte
– urlava –
non ti fermare!
Il nostro destino
non è ancora scritto:
il cuore
ha un ultimo battito
da officiare!»
Il crinale del monte
era lì a due passi
a segnare
l'ultimo volo della civetta.
E la mente
si librò nel vortice
d'infiniti dilemmi,
senza eco
e senza risposta...

Ma improvvise
risplendettero di luce
nella notte
le tue pupille;
invisibili ali
mi abbracciarono
nel silenzio assoluto
delle palpitanti stelle...

«Shout louder
– he screamed –
do not stop!
Our destiny
is not yet written:
the heart
has one last beat
to officiate!"
The ridge of the mountain
was there just a few steps away
to mark
the last flight of the owl.
And the mind
freed itself in the vortex
of infinite dilemmas,
without echo
and without response...

But suddenly
your pupils
shone with light
in the night;
invisible wings
embraced me
in the absolute silence
of the palpitating stars...

Sconcerto di musiche acquarelli.
Ondeggiano a primavera capelli,
quali serti rapiti di Alloro,
dalla tepida carezza d'Apollo.

Al veleggiare di stormi migranti
la morte ci apparirà allo Zenit,
vicina icona e indaco crepuscolo,
immacolata alba e lontana effige:
glorioso elmo nuziale di Dafne.

Sei sicura dell'eternità
che fragile ancora inquieta la vita?

Inutile ti respiro sorridente al sole?

O sei la Veronica che germoglia silente
al palpito dell'iride celeste,
al primo scroscio di pioggia
sul limitar del sentiero dorato?

The bewilderment of watercolored music.
Hair billows in Spring,
like stolen laurel wreaths,
from the warm caress of Apollo.

At the gliding of flocks of migrants
death will appear to us at the Zenith,
a nearby icon and indigo twilight,
immaculate dawn and distant effigy:
Daphne's glorious wedding helmet.

Are you sure of eternity
which, fragile still, perturbs life?

Needlessly do I breathe you in, smiling at the sun?

Or are you the Veronica[4] that silently sprouts
at the pulse of the celestial iris,
at the first shower of rain
at the edge of the golden path?

Catturati
nel dolce
cullarsi
sul vuoto.

Sii clemente!

Non posso dividere
col tutto
il niente.

Ma vorrei
almeno
capissi
che l'ho tentato.

Captured
while sweetly
rocking
over the void.

Be kind!

I cannot share
this nothingness
with everything.

But I wish
at least
you understood
that I tried.

Corbula fossile del Madagascar

Ho chiesto a quest'umile corbula
chi la raccolse ormai fossile da sì lontani lidi:
«un piccone senza cuore – rispose –
mi divelse dalla roccia marina
ed ora rammento il tempo passato
ad ascoltare il mare senza parlare.
Era quello un destino forse migliore
che rimaner qui a consolare
un rudere d'uomo barcollante nel buio
del più sottil vaniloquio... ».

Corbula, a fossil from Madagascar[5]

I asked this humble corbula who had gathered her,
now a fossil, from such distant shores:
«A heartless pickaxe», she answered,
«uprooted me from the sea rock
and now I recall the time I spent
listening to the sea without speaking.
That was perhaps a better fate
than to remain here to console
a ruin of a man staggering in the darkness
of the subtlest nonsensical discourse... ».

«Carpe diem!»

L'orizzonte pullula fosco
di navigli condotti alla deriva
da onde incontinenti,
duri da governare come le menti
di una lercia genìa di gaudenti,
nel salso brago intenti
al sol dell'apparire.

Carpe diem!

Falsamente qualcuno lo interpretò
grugnendo grafi in teli di lino:
altre spiagge ed altri templi
stralunavano allora.
Mentre ora dalle tasche
ogni quattrino s'invola
senza tracce
per adorare
le notturne stelle
del sabato divino.

«Carpe diem!»

The horizon swarms darkly
with ships drifting
from incontinent waves,
hard to govern like the minds
of a filthy generation of revelers,
in the salty mire intent
upon the sun of appearances.

Carpe diem!

Falsely someone interpreted it
by grunting scratches in linen cloths:
other shores and other temples
led people astray in those times.
While now every penny flies
from the pockets
leaving no trace,
to adore
the nocturnal stars
of the divine Sabbath.

Gocce d'acqua
su leggieri sentieri d'alte vette,
luminosi sguardi
di semplici terre in attesa
raccontano
amor fuggito e ritrovato:
lassù dove i cieli si confondono
fra boschi crepitanti nell'aria,
così densi di sogni inverati.

Si vive
ormai certi nel sole
a ricamare questo giorno
già gravido di luce.

Fila il Tessitor
paziente la vita,
tingendoci negli occhi
colori impensati,
sì che l'immagine tua splendente,
la notte disvela
nell'iride mia così impressa
da riconoscerne,
vivente nel fondo,

Drops of water
on light trails of high peaks,
bright views
upon simple lands waiting,
they tell
of love avoided and found again:
up there where the skies blend
in with the woods crackling in the air,
so rich in dreams that have come true.

Now we live
certain in the sun
embroidering this day
already pregnant with light.

Patiently the Weaver
spins life,
dyeing our eyes
with unimaginable colors,
so that your shining image,
does the night unveil
in my iris so impressed
as to recognize in it,
living in the depths,

il chiaro Amore
che guiderà
il valzer futuro.

the clear Love
that will guide
the coming waltz.

Cirri nel cielo,
sussulti del tempo che s'invola,
presagio della fine irreversibile
dei tuoi capelli intrecciati di fiabe,
del tuo e nostro universo.

E poi...

        ...rigirarsi gli occhi verso l'interno!

Demenze in contrappasso
a pensieri che superano inumani
la soglia dell'indicibile.

Eppur continuo a vivere stupito
la non linearità dell'orizzonte
che pulsa dentro ogni nuovo amplesso
(un nuovo inganno?!):
testo inestricabile,
ragnatela ritessuta con caparbia
da cuori malati di tempo.

Oppure...

        ... improvvisa tresca d'Agàpe

Cirrus clouds in the sky,
tremors of time that flies away,
foretaste of the irreversible end
of your hair entwined with fairy tales,
of your and our universe.

And then...
                    ...turn your eyes inward!

Dementias in contrast
with thoughts that, inhuman,
exceed the threshold of the unspeakable.

And yet I continue to be amazed
at the non-linearity of the horizon
that pulsates within every new copulation
(a new deception?!):
inextricable text,
cobweb re-woven stubbornly
from hearts sick of time.

Or perhaps...
                    ...a sudden affair of Agàpe

ritmata da rovi
e condotta da Chi,
appeso a due assi perpendicoli di legno,
ricongiunge i cardini del Cosmo
e recide il nodo gordiano
del ferino ballo mimetico,
casto lasciandosi sgozzare:
il Logos-Sangue versato,
insufflato Spirito,
finalmente illumina
questa spelonca d'ombre
irriflesse d'eterno!

whose rhythm is set by brambles

and conducted by One who,

hanging on two perpendicular wooden planks,

rejoins the cornerstones of the Cosmos

and cuts the Gordian knot

of the feral camouflaged dance,

chaste, allowing himself to be slaughtered:

the Logos-Blood poured out,

insufflated Spirit,

finally illuminates

this cavern with spontaneous

shadows of the eternal!

All'alba vidi giungere una donna,
che mi destò dal dormiveglia e spense,
con improvvisa folata di gonna,
il pianto mio intriso in fobìe dense.

Non persi amplessi per diva vendetta,
ma il mio cuore in notti alchemiche
s'immerse nella Fonte d'Alta Vetta,
che sana al Sole anime anemiche.

Vedi Tu e cura le ferite labili,
nate al ritmo e al ticchettìo dell'ora,
convulsa in baci e strette improbabili,

ove Eros mi donò fatua corona.
Sei nel profondo silenzio ancora
la mia unica Speranza àfona...

Mystic dance

At dawn I saw a woman come,
who woke me from my half-sleep and stopped,
with a sudden lash of her skirt,
my weeping soaked in dense fears.

I did not miss amorous embraces for a godly vendetta,
but my heart in alchemic nights
plunged into the Source of Great Heights,
which heals anemic souls in the Sun.

See and cure the ephemeral wounds,
born to the rhythm and the ticking of the hour,
convulsed in improbable kisses and embraces,

where Eros gave me a fatuous crown.
You are in the deep silence still
my only unvoiced Hope...

POESIE DI EMANUELE SARTORI

«Meravigliosa Grazia! Che Lieta Novella
che ha salvato un miserabile come me!
Un tempo ero perduto, ma ora sono ritrovato.
Ero cieco, ma ora ci vedo.

È stata la Grazia ad insegnare al mio cuore il timor di Dio
ed è la Grazia che mi solleva dalla paura;
quanto preziosa mi apparve quella Grazia
nell'ora in cui ho cominciato a credere!

Attraverso molti pericoli, travagli e insidie
sono già passato;
la Grazia mi ha condotto in salvo fin qui,
e la Grazia mi condurrà a casa.

Il Signore mi ha promesso il Bene,
la sua Parola sostiene la mia Speranza;
Egli sarà la mia difesa e la mia eredità,
per tutta la durata della vita.

Sì, quando questa carne e questo cuore verranno meno,
e la vita mortale cesserà,
io entrerò in possesso, oltre il velo,
di una Vita di Gioia e di Pace»[6].

Poems by Emanuele Sartori

«Amazing Grace! What a Good News
that saved a wretch like me!
I once was lost, but now am found
T'was blind, but now I see.

T'was Grace that taught my heart to fear
and Grace my fears relieved
How precious did that Grace appear
The hour I first believed!

Through many dangers, toils and snares
We have already come.
T'was grace that brought us safe thus far
And grace will lead us home.

The Lord has promised good to me,
His word my hope secures;
He will my Shield and Portion be,
As long as life endures.

Yes, when this flesh and heart shall fail,
And mortal life shall cease,
I shall possess, within the veil,
a Life of Joy and Peace»[7].

Sei Tu Signore il motore.
Io le ali.

Comanda ai tuoi venti la rotta
e fammi volare nella gioia
del tuo volere.

Libero di amare e di sorridere
come aria nel vento,
grazie al soffio del tuo Spirito.

You Lord are the engine.
I the wings.

Command your winds the route
and let me fly in the joy
of your will.

Free to love and smile
like air in the wind,
thanks to the breath of your Spirit.

È rinato
in ogni uomo creato,
che, se non è amato,
ha il cuore spezzato.

La croce Lo ha innalzato
perché io dovevo essere curato.

Ho cercato l'Amore
e l'ho trovato con stupore
e senza malumore.

Gesù è tornato
in un sorriso donato.
Ogni vivente
che è credente
può affermare:
«a Dio devo tornare!
Nel suo cuore dimorare
e la felicità ritrovare!»

He is reborn
in every created man, who,
if he is not loved,
has a broken heart.

The cross lifted Him up
because I had to be cured.

I looked for Love
and found it in amazement
and without discontent.

Jesus has returned
in the gift of a smile.
Every living being
that believes
can affirm:
«I must return to God!
To dwell in his heart
and find happiness again!»

Che cos'è che porta frutto
se non quello che va bevuto
in un calice innalzato...

...in un banchetto prelibato?

Senza peccato ricevuto.
Lì ove trovi il Tutto.

Eucharist

What is it that bears fruit
if not what is to be drunk
in a raised chalice...

        ...in a delicious banquet?

Received without sin.
There where you find the All.

Oggi è nato
Chi doveva nascere
per sempre beato
nel suo trono dorato
e tutti possono credere
che l'Amore si può toccare
e con la Fede gustare.

Today is born
He who had to be born[8]
forever blessed
in his golden throne[9]
and everyone can believe
that Love can be touched
and with Faith be tasted[10].

Gesù: IO SONO la Luce vera
           che porta la primavera.

Gesù: Quando qualcuno mi ferisce
           con un sasso mi colpisce.

Emanuele: Senza di Te non ce la faccio
           e va a finire che spaccio.

Gesù: Mi devi capire:
           la tristezza deve sparire.

Emanuele: Ma come fare?
           Mi devo sparare?

Gesù: No! Sono IO che ti cambio.
           Il tuo vestito con il mio ti scambio.

Emanuele: Perché morire?
           E tante volte soffrire?

Gesù: Se a me ti affidi,
           e nel dubbio confidi
           che IO SONO la Luce,
           il tuo venir meno frutto produce!

Jesus: I AM the true Light
              that brings Spring.

Jesus: When someone wounds me,
              he strikes me with a rock.

Emanuele: Without you I can't do it
              and I'll end up selling[11].

Jesus: You have to understand me:
              sadness must disappear.

Emanuele: But how to do it?
              Should I shoot myself?

Jesus: No! It is I who change you.
              I exchange your clothes for mine[12].

Emanuele: Why die?
              And suffer so many times?

Jesus: If you entrust yourself to me,
              and when in doubt, trust
              that I AM the Light,
              your failing produces fruit!

AMORE

LOVE

Che bello quel sorriso!
che dovunque vada
mi porta il paradiso
e fa in modo che non cada
in una tristezza fatale
che sembra un funerale.

Sono tanto felice
che questo dono elargito
non provenga da un'attrice
dal volto incupito.

Ma dal Signore,
che ti guarisce meglio di un dottore
l'angoscia infernale,
quale una ferita mortale.

Devi sapere che
questo sorriso
non ha un perché.

È un dono gratuito
che non è stato pattuito.

How nice – that smile!
that everywhere I go,
brings me heaven,
and ensures I don't fall
into a fatal sadness
that feels like a funeral.

I am so happy
that this gift given
doesn't come from an actress
with a clouded face.

But from the Lord,
Who heals you better than a doctor
from the infernal anguish,
like a mortal wound.

You should know that
there's no reason
behind this smile.

It is a free gift
that wasn't negotiated on.

Ma la più bella cosa
è che:
questa rima non è una prosa
e se provocherà un sorriso
avrà lo splendore del paradiso!

But the best thing
is that:
This rhyme is not prose
and if it causes a smile,
it will have the splendor of heaven!

Paradiso

Tutto il mondo risuona
dell'Alleluia pasquale,
senza il quale
la bellezza stona.

Devi sapere che
Cristo ha dato un perché
a quella sensazione
che ti dà una bella emozione,
come quando guardi il creato
con il cor innamorato
di una bellezza nuova
che in Dio si trova.

«Spezza le catene del peccato,
e quello che ho detto, sarà tuo!»
Il sole non sarà mai tramontato.

Tu e Dio sarete un perfetto duo.
Il tuo vestito senza macchia sarà.
Il tuo nuovo cuore sarà suo.

Il paradiso apre le porte.

Paradise

The whole world resonates
with the Easter alleluia,
without which
beauty is out of tune.

You should know that
Christ has given a reason
for that sensation
that creates a beautiful emotion within you,
like when you look at creation
with your heart in love
with a new beauty
that is found in God.

«Break the chains of sin,
and what I have said, will be yours!»
The sun will never set.

You and God will be a perfect duo.
Your clothing will be spotless.
Your new heart will be his.

Paradise opens its doors.

L'uomo di ieri è passato
e il cancello è chiuso alla morte.

Se la fiamma si spegne,
ravvivala con nuove gemme.

L'amore si alzerà
e il sole ritornerà.

The man of yesterday is past
and the gate is closed to death.

If the flame keeps going out,
revive it with new gems.

Love will rise
and the Sun will return.

Sono vivo
pieno di gioia nel cuore
per dar lode al Creatore.
Per questo scrivo!

La Verità
è un profumo intenso.
E, se la ripenso,
è la TRINITÁ.

La vita deve stare
ad ammirare
una nuova luce
che Gesù produce
per chi crede
e non cede,
in disaccordo col Verbo,
a un frutto acerbo,
che dai demoni
è stato maledetto,
ma predetto
da un posto non transitorio,
su cui è seduto
Chi è stato creduto.

Charity

I'm alive
full of joy in my heart
to give praise to the Creator.
For this I write!

The Truth
is an intense perfume.
And, to think about it,
it's the TRINITY.

Life must
admire
a new light
that Jesus produces
for the one who believes[13]
and who does not yield[14],
disagreeing with the Word,
over a bitter fruit[15],
that by the Devil
has been cursed[16],
but foretold[17]
from a non-transitory place,
upon which is seated
He who has been believed[18].

Viene un'alba nuova,
con un impeto creatore
sale dall'infinito
una Luce d'oro zecchino,
che riveste il mondo
di un abbraccio d'amore.

A new dawn is coming,
with a creating thrust
there rises from the infinite[19]
a Light[20] of pure gold,
that covers the world
in a loving embrace.

L'amore è delizioso
ed è molto prezioso
perché a nessuno dispiace
quando è una fornace
che il male consuma
e tutto profuma.

Love is delicious
and is very precious,
because no one minds
when it is a furnace
that consumes evil
and perfumes everything.

La Morte

THE DEATH

Allo spegnersi dell'ultimo raggio
rivedo la mia vita
che oramai è perita;

lascio tutto
all'addiaccio...
        ...non porto nulla:
mi trovo giusto
e vedrò quanto gusto
quando l'Amore mi culla.

Death

At the dying of the last ray
I look back on my life
which by now has perished;

I leave everything
to that terrible goodbye...

                ...I don't bring anything with me:

I feel right
and know how I'll enjoy it
when Love cradles me.

Il paradiso è riempito,
di una gioia intriso
per un uomo arrivato,
morto il giorno preciso,
in cui tutto è compiuto,
come prima del tempo
il vestito cucito
«per sempre nel Mio grembo».

Paradise is filled,
and imbued with joy
for a man who's arrived,
died that same day,
in which all has been fulfilled,
like before time[21]
the sown garment[22]
«always in My womb».

Senza crudeltà
mi sono ritrovato
rinnovato nella carità
con il peccato cancellato.

Without cruelty[23]
I found myself
renewed in charity,
and my sins cancelled.

Una stella nuova nel firmamento del Cielo

Danza l'Aquilone
sotto lo sguardo di mille occhi.
Lui vola per amare.

Una nuova luce risplende
in un cielo terso d'Amore.
Le nuvole sono cupe
ma trasparenti.

Il Cielo è germinato
da una danza nuziale.

P.S.: *Sono estremamente felice.*

A new star in the firmament of Heaven

The Kite Dances
beneath the gaze of a thousand eyes.
He flies in order to love.

A new light shines
in a clear sky of Love.
The clouds are dark
but transparent.

Heaven has sprouted
from a wedding dance.

P.S. *I am extremely happy.*

L'Amore trionfa

Love triumphs

Ciò che era
è rimasto.
Senza traccia
se n'è andato
il peccato.
La battaglia
è cessata.

Una nuova era
è incominciata.
Niente è perduto,
ma riavuto.

Il Sole è rinnovato
da un infinito Amore
che in dolce tepore
riscalda il cuore.

Tutto esiste
in un nuovo colore.

Il silenzio è nel cuore
terso dal dolore,

What was[24]
has remained.
Sin
is gone
without a trace.
The battle
has ceased.

A new era
has begun.
Nothing is lost,
but rather is possessed anew.

The Sun is renewed
by an infinite Love
which in gentle warmth
warms the heart.

Everything exists
in a new color.

There is silence in the heart
freed of pain, but full of peace.

ma colmo di pace.
Nuovi orizzonti
s'intravvedono
di spazi infiniti...

    ...l'Amore trionfa!

New horizons
are glimpsed,
with infinite spaces...

                    ...Love triumphs!

Se Dio tace
è perché il suo cuore è una brace
che di vane parole non si compiace.

Ma la lingua di Dio
è il creato
che in un silenzio spietato
così è stato preparato;
siccome tu devi capire
che a qualcosa di più grande devi ardire.

E la vita perde il suo perché
se non c'è
questa frase piena di significato
con chi ti ha creato.

Relation. I. You.

If God is silent
It is because his heart is all embers
that do not take pleasure in vain words.

But the language of God
is creation
that in a ruthless quiet[25]
has been prepared;
since you have to understand
that you must aspire to something greater[26].

And life loses its meaning
if this phrase full of sense
with the one who created you,
should be lacking.

Dio parla

Se ti crucci sui tuoi pensieri
la mente ritorna a ieri.
Perché continuare a flagellarsi?
Devi sapere che con Dio cambi!
Ma per un abbraccio le spalle devono girarsi;
basta con il demonio scambi.

«Se vuoi reagire
una mano IO ti tendo,
perché a te protendo
un'eternità senza perire».

God speaks

If you worry over your thoughts,
the mind goes back to yesterday.
Why continue to flagellate yourself?
You should know that with God you change!
But to give a hug, you have to turn back around;
enough speaking with the devil[27].

«If you want to react,
I offer you my hand,
since I proffer you
an eternity without perishing».

IO ho inviato la Luce apparsa nel mondo
che porta in sé ogni dolcezza;
se ti sembra di cambiare il globo rotondo
devi sapere che lo colmi solo di asprezza,
perché ciò che muta proviene dall'Immutabile
e quelle che fai tu sono solo chiacchiere,
mentre la mia lingua è amabile
come il ghiaccio d'estate in un bicchiere.

L'amore vero, IO lo dono,
se tu chiedi il mio perdono.
E tutta la Terra si riempie
di una fragranza nuova
perché il tuo recipiente
un nuovo colore trova.

Ma se tu manchi di umiltà
si abbassa la carità.
Perché l'*Assoluto* così è fatto:
pieno di senso nel suo agire
con un nuovo aroma nel dire
come un cibo prelibato.

I have sent the Light which appeared in the world,
which bears within it all sweetness;
if you feel you'll change the whole round world,
you must know that you only fill it with bitterness,
because what changes comes from the Un-changing One
and what you do is only chatter,
while my tongue is as pleasant
as ice in the glass in summer.

True love, I give it,
if you ask for my forgiveness.
And the whole Earth is filled
with a new fragrance
so that your receptacle
takes on a new color.

But if you lack humility,
charity is lessened.
Because thus is the *Absolute:*
thoughtful in his actions,
with a new aroma in his words,
like a choice dish.

Siamo immersi in un abisso di bontà.

Abyss

We are immersed in an abyss of goodness.

Luce d'Eterna Luce,
splendi più che mai!

Senza tramonto
irradia il mio cuore!

Cosicché
io viva di Te.

Light of Eternal Light,
shine more than ever!

Irradiate my heart
with a light that never sets!

So
may I live from You.

Ho visto Dio.
Era molto grato,
siccome mi sono trovato
rinato in un nuovo io.

La Luce era raggiante.
Le sue Parole frecce
sgorgate da tre Facce
di una Sapienza abbagliante.

I have seen God.
He was very grateful,
since I found myself
reborn in a new self[28].

The Light was radiant.
His Words, arrows
gushing from three Faces
with a dazzling Wisdom.

Sono pieno di luce
che frutto produce,
in un nuovo mondo
in cui mio Figlio
ha seminato un Giglio
in molte anime fecondo,
che nella Santa Messa
la sua bellezza si è espressa.

I am full of light
that produces fruit,
in a new world
in which my Son
has sown a Lily[29]
in many fruitful souls,
for in the Holy Mass
his beauty is expressed.

Posso
e distruggo
chi voglio
e quando voglio.

Non temo nulla
e non devo temere
perché il mio Nome è potente,
degno di un RE,
che non pensa mai
a chi si oppone,
ma scuote i rami
per far cadere
i frutti marci,
che dell'inferno
hanno il sapore.

Se IO sapessi calcolare
quanto valgo,
i numeri cadrebbero
perché inconsistenti.

Lord of Hosts

I have the power
and I destroy
whom I want
and when I want.

I fear nothing
and I do not have to fear
for my Name is powerful,
worthy of a KING,
who never thinks
of those who object,
but shakes the branches
to cause to fall
the rotten fruit,
which have the taste
of Hell.

If I knew how to calculate
how much I'm worth,
the numbers would fail
because they wouldn't add up.

Se posso fare
non aspetto,
perché brucio
di un Fuoco
inestinguibile.

Domenica, 27 settembre 2015

In memoriam del maleficio
spezzato dalla Milizia Celeste.

If I am able,
I don't wait,
because I burn
with an inextinguishable
Fire.

Sunday, September 27, 2015

In memoriam of the course
broken by the Heavenly Militia

Beata Vergine Maria

«*Regina sine labe originale concepta*»

Blessed Virgin Mary

«*Regina sine labe originale concepta*»[30]

Maria!

Una mamma in Cielo ti assiste,
perché per te esiste
e i più bei desideri
li fa volare come pensieri,
fino a dove si baciano
e un cammino ti tracciano.

Mary!

A mother in Heaven assists you,
because she exists for you
and the most beautiful desires
she makes fly like thoughts,
until they kiss
and trace out a path.

Sono rinato
perché accompagnato,
senz'altra guida o luce
fuor di quella che nel cor mi riluce.

Triste me ne andavo
ma a Gesù pensavo.

Mia sorella Maria,
stupefatta del mio operato,
con un sorriso donato:
sotto il suo manto
un cammino ho iniziato!

Smile!

I am reborn
because I'm accompanied,
with no other guide or light
save that which shines within my heart.

I was going around sad,
but I was thinking of Jesus.

My sister Mary,
bewildered by my actions,
with a gifted smile:
under her mantle
I began a journey!

Tu sei la più bella
del firmamento la stella,
che guida i cuori
verso Dio, e gli onori.
Dappertutto ammirata
mai trascurata,
perché importante,
per sempre Maria la Clemente.

Mary the Clement

You are the most beautiful
star in the firmament,
which guides hearts
towards God, and you honor them.
Everywhere admired
never neglected,
because you are important,
always Mary the Clement.

In Cammino verso il Cielo

On the Road to Heaven

Canto del Pellegrino

La vita è rinata
da un'acqua sognata
intrisa d'amore
che con stupore
allevia il dolore
a chi percorre
un duro sentiero,
cui occorre
contro 'l nemico
un gentile guerriero,
che per mezzo del Sacrificio,
con amore elargito,
ci rende il cuore contrito
per respingere
chi fa tacere
l'Amore
Consolatore.

In onore della B. V. Maria
per l'acqua di Lourdes,
di San Michele Arcangelo
e del Sacrificio Eucaristico

The truth is reborn
from a dreamt-of water
imbued with love
that with wonder
alleviates the pain
of those who travel
a hard path,
which requires
against the enemy
a gentle warrior,
who by means of Sacrifice,
with love bequeathed,
makes our heart contrite
to reject
he who silences
the Consoling
Love.

In honor of the B. V. Mary
for the water of Lourdes,
of St. Michael Archangel
and of the Eucharistic Sacrifice

Per chi non crede, il cui cuore cede

Oggi sono riuscito ad amare
perché la salvezza devo lucrare.
Sono io che esisto
ma nel pensiero di Dio preesisto.

Ogni vita va creata
ma la sorte non deve essere rovinata.

Io desidero essere amato
ma il cordone ombelicale deve essere tagliato.

Se il minuto che passa
se la spassa,
Dio un pugno incassa.
Senza contare che
al minuto non ho dato un perché!

La vita è bella
se alle lacrime non bisogna mettere l'ombrella.

Se tu vuoi capire,
Dio, nel tuo cuore, deve investire!

For he who does not believe, the heart gives way

Today I managed to love
because I must profit from salvation.
It is I who exist
but in the mind of God I pre-exist.

Each life must be created
but its lot must not be ruined.

I desire to be loved
but the umbilical cord must be cut[31].

If one spends poorly
the minute that passes,
God takes a punch[32].
Without considering that
I have not even given a reason to the minute!

Life is beautiful
if you needn't take out an umbrella for your tears.

If you wish to understand,
you must invest God in your heart!

Ma quello che mi preme
è che se ami, la vita si spreme,
in un bel calice di succo;
ma se odi, bevi da una coppa
che è bella quanto un trucco!

But what urges me
is that if you love, life is squeezed,
into a beautiful glass of juice;
but if you hate, you drink from a cup
that's no more pleasant than a trick!

Ti devi spogliare
perché quando Dio parla
la tua mente libera deve stare
siccome c'è chi di te sparla.

Ma alla fine della vita
di ogni parola proferita
l'essenza è perita.

Se non che, l'Essere
imprime la sua sostanza
in ogni frase che ti fa crescere
e che ti ridona la speranza.

You must undress yourself
because when God speaks
your mind must be free
since there's one who speaks badly of you[33].

But at the end of life
of every word proffered,
the essence has perished.

If not for the fact that, Being
imprints its substance
in every phrase that makes you grow
and gives you back hope.

La Speranza non tace
e al demonio dispiace.

La gioia è sepolta
perché l'anima è incolta.

Devi trovare
la gioia da cavalcare,
che fino in Paradiso ti deve portare.

E' una speranza vera
che ti dà il profumo di primavera,
quella che dà senso al tuo perché.

Hope will not be silent
and the Devil does not like this.

Joy is buried
because the soul is uncultured.

You must find
the joy to ride,
for it must carry you to Heaven.

It is a true hope
that gives you the perfume of Spring,
that gives a meaning to your question.

Trova il fato,
uomo peccatore!
Non è un piatto prelibato.
Né un felice dottore.

Mentre è un velo dorato
il cammino della Provvidenza,
pieno di sapienza
in un silenzio celato.

Find fate,
sinful man!
It is not a choice dish.
Nor a happy doctor.

While a golden veil[34]
is the way of Providence,
full of wisdom
hidden in silence.

Quando guardo il Sole
che illumina la prole,
provo smarrimento.
Tipo un tradimento.
E mi dico:
la mia mente ha un attrito!
Non riesco a capire!
Chi mi può tradire?
Questo fato
da dove può venire?
Può essere creato?
Dio non mi può tradire!
Il mio non senso si esprime
in una frustrazione da patire.

Ma Dio mi imprime
tante cose da scoprire.
Provo ad immaginare.
Dove devo cercare?
Chi mi può chiamare?
In questo lago di asprezza
che ogni uomo disprezza,
chi mi viene incontro?

When I look at the Sun[35]
that illumines the offspring[36],
I feel bewildered.
Almost like a betrayal[37].
And I say to myself:
my mind has failed![38]
I can't understand!
Who could betray me?
From whence could
this fate come?
Can it be created?
God cannot betray me!
My non-sense is expressed
in frustration to be suffered.

But God impresses upon me
so many things to be discovered.
I try to imagine.
Where must I seek?
Who can call me?[39]
In this lake of bitterness
that every man despises,
who will come to my aid?

Per farmi riscoprire
una porta da aprire
su qualcos'Altro:
lì una novella Luce
dalle tenebre mi conduce
su un orizzonte
da cui scaturisce
una nuova Fonte,
dove la bellezza non perisce.

To help me rediscover
a door to open
onto something Else:
there a new Light
leads me out of the darkness
onto a horizon
from which
a new Spring flows,
where beauty does not perish.

Sono tornato
di una beltà innamorato.
Il seme è germogliato,
che nel mio cor incentrato
è stato preparato
da Chi mi ha creato.

I have returned
from a beauty in love.
The seed has sprouted,
which, centered in my heart,
was prepared
by Him who created me.

L'Amore è vivo
per me che perivo
ed è più creativo
di una noia mortale
che sempre mi assale.

Love is alive for me
for I was perishing
and is more creative
than the crushing boredom
that always assails me.[40]

Il patto è stato violato.
In un modo così acerbo.
L'umanità ha peccato.

In disaccordo col Verbo
un portale hanno aperto
in un modo così superbo.

Niente è più certo:
il giardino è murato.
Tutto rimane deserto.

The pact has been broken.[41]
In so embittered a fashion.
Humanity has sinned.

Disagreeing with the Word,
they have opened a portal[42]
in so proud a fashion.[43]

Nothing is certain anymore[44]:
the garden is walled in.
All remains deserted.

Io spero
e in Te credo
e non cedo
in ciò che ero.

Per dar gusto
a Chi mi ha salvato,
per Lui creato
in un cammino angusto.

I hope
and I believe in You
and I do not give way
to what I was.

To please
the One who has saved me,
created for Him
in a narrow way.

Sono vivo
e sempre rinato
da un pianto
sul mio volto inciso.

Può servire
questo lacrimare?
I peccati devo espiare
e un sì ogni dì ridire.

My yes

I am alive
and always reborn
from weeping
carved upon my face.

Can these tears
be of use?
I must expiate my sins
and re-pronounce my yes every day.

Dai fiumi scende la neve
senz'altra meta
che la terra stanca,
perduta nel vento
di molte battaglie.

Alla deriva
quest'acqua chiara
perde il suo senno
in chi male spera.
Nulla trova
dove egli abita.

Senza naufragar
quest'acqua chiara
trova la strada,
che di tante fatiche
si compiace.

Più candida
di mille stelle pare.
Il massimo vuole
per baciare il cuore

Down there

Snow falls from the rivers[45]
with no other scope
than the tired earth,
lost in the wind
of many battles.

Drifting[46]
this clear water[47]
loses its mind
in he who hopes for evil.
It finds nothing
where he dwells.[48]

Without shipwrecking,
this clear water
finds the road,[49]
that is pleased
with many hardships.

It seems brighter
than a thousand stars.[50]
It desires the utmost,
to kiss the heart[51]

di un bianco colorato.
Trova la sua penna
chi di luce scrive
la sua vita innamorata.

colored in white.[52]
He finds his pen[53]
who writes in light[54]
his enamored life.[55]

Questo universo è soltanto una virgola
di una Divina Commedia futura.

This universe is only a comma
of a future Divine Comedy.

Gioia

Attimi di eternità:
sorrido...

Joy

Moments of eternity:
I smile…

«Ianua Coeli»

Lieto nella sofferenza
da Cristo imparo,
nel cuore una Presenza,
che il destino amaro
tutto trasforma
e di senso impregna.

Sotto una nuova forma
il futuro ridisegna.

SANTA FE, 07 July 2016,
4:00 PM (ACI Stampa).

Sister Cecilia Maria has been nick-named *the nun of the smile*. She was a nun from the Discalced Carmel-ite Monastery in Santa Fe, Argen-tina, and her smiling photo, before she died, went around the world on all social networks. There was a great deal of sharing in that smile that welcomed death (the Life *ndr*) on 23 June 2016, at the age of 42. (*V. Giacometti*).

Joyful in suffering
I learn from Christ,
a Presence in the heart,
that bitter destiny
entirely transforms[56]
and imbues with meaning.

It redraws the future[57]
in a new shape.

NOTES

1   Cf. Francesco Sartori, *Naked Castaways between Samos and Patmos* [*Ignudi naufraghi fra Samo e Patmos*] (Phasar, Florence, 2003).

2   St. Theresa of Jesus (of Avila), mystic, reformer and doctor of the Catholic Church. Translation: "Let nothing disturb you, / let nothing afflict you; / everything passes, / God never changes; / patience / obtains all things; / he who has God / lacks nothing. / God alone is enough".

3   Fr. Leone was the spiritual director of the author Francesco and his exorcist. He helped him discover the love of Jesus, Joseph and Mary, drawing him out of a state of intellectual agnosticism, existential atheism, familial, socio-political, and moral rebellion, with an anarchic-radical type of active anti-Christian militancy. All this was leading Francesco into the darkness of despair, serious depression, some forms of addiction and dabbling in the occult. Thanks to the help and prayers of Fr. Leone and to his mother's tears (R.I.P.) - a new St. Monica - he gradually arrived, by impervious ways and not without stumbling, at Faith in the Way, Truth and Life: Jesus the Liberator! He still is holding him by the hand and always lifts him up... He loved him first! Infinite thanks to the God of all Mercies and to the Blessed Virgin Mary, Mother of God, mediatrix of all Graces!

4   Veronica manifests itself as a group of very small blue flowers that color the fields throughout the year; its scientific name is Veronica persica, but it is known by all as «occhi della Madonna» (the *Madonna's Eyes*). The meaning of the name Veronica from the Greek is I bring victory; indeed, it seems that they can heal various illnesses, it is even thought that this might be traced back to the name of the woman who, wiping the face of Christ during the Via Crucis, was able to alleviate his wounds; some see this name as deriving from the Latin *vera* et *unica*. But in the language of flowers, the Veronica flower signifies goodbye, and at one time it used to be given to a friend who was about to leave, with the hope that the divine eyes would always watch over and follow one's dear one (but this is not to be confused with the *Myosotis*, better known as the *forget-me-not*). A beautiful story is linked to this flower and recounts the origin of the name of the *Madonna's eyes:*

> «One beautiful morning, in Malcantone (Canton Ticino, Switzerland, ed.) the Madonna descended with her child, to enjoy our springtime. The Madonna was

153

walking along a sloping path, watching over her child,
who was running happily among the grass and flowers.
After a while, the child Jesus was thirsty and asked for
a drink. The Mother looked around, and listened, but
not a drop of water flowed. She was about to pick up
her child and go back up to heaven, when a little white
flower caught her eye which, in the shadow of a random
block of stone, almost did not dare to show itself. The
Madonna drew close to the flower, plucked it, and saw
inside that paleness a drop of dew, which shone with light
like a diamond. She held the flower like out a miniature
cup to the little one's lips, so that he might drink the dew.
Jesus' thirst was slaked and once more he began to run
in the grass. The Virgin comforted the poor flower with
a glance, as its head was bent over upon its stalk. She
brought it back to the shadow of the rock, reattaching it
miraculously to the stem. Soon the flower straightened up
and became blue like the iris of the Madonna, who had
glanced at it for a moment. And all the flowers of that
species dyed their white petals in a delicate blue. From that
time onwards, in Malcantone, veronicas are called «little
Madonna's eyes»; they peek out in springtime from the
paths, from the banks of streams, as flowers sacred to the
«Alma Mater Coelorum» (Chiesa Virgilio, *L'anima del*
villaggio, Gaggini, Lugano, 1934)*: cf* Valeria Bonora
in *www.eticamente.net/49317/la-ieggenda-degii-occhi-*
della-madonna.htm.

5   *Corbula,* fossil of Madagascar of the family of *Corbulids,*
characterized by the fact that one of their valves is smaller than the
other. Moreover, their valves are so strong that they are preyed upon
only with difficulty. It has a silky *periostracum.* It lives in sandy seabeds.

1.2 cm in size. Fairly common (from Wikipedia).

6   Poems written by the Author Emanuele from September 2015
to January 2017. *Amazing Grace* by John Newton (late 18th century).
Translation by Authors.

7   John Newton, Amazing Grace (end of the 18th century).

Poems written by Emanuele from September 2015 to January 2017.

8   Jesus of Nazareth is born, the Christ or Messiah foretold by
the Jewish tradition and beyond (see the adoration of the "Three
Kings").

9   The Ascension: *The Lord Jesus, after speaking with them, was assumed into heaven and was seated at the right hand of God;* Mark 16:19; cf. Luke 24:50-52.

10   The Eucharistic gift that takes place in every Holy Sacrifice of the Mass.

11   Selling drugs.

12   The soul has its own garment. God gives you his royal garment to celebrate with Him.

13   In Your Light we see Light.

14   And who does not sin.

15   The knowledge of good and, above all, of evil indicated in Genesis as the forbidden fruit of the Garden or earthly Paradise.

16   The first sin, cursed by Lucifer, was afterwards sung by the Church as *Felix Culpa* (as St. Ambrose first defined it), since it merited for us the Incarnation of the Word and thus Redemption. The expression is contained in the *Exsultet*: (in the Missals before 1920 it was written *Exultet*) it is a liturgical song proper to the Catholic Church which is sung the night of Easter in the solemn Easter vigil. With it, the victory of Light over the darkness is proclaimed, symbolized by the paschal candle that is lit, and announces the Resurrection of Christ; the one singing invites the whole assembly to rejoice for the fulfillment of the prophecy of the Paschal Mystery, retracing in the song the marvels of the history of salvation (from *Wikipedia*).

17   God, before original sin, had foretold that if they ate of that forbidden fruit Adam and Eve would die.

18   God, or rather the Eternal Word of the Father became incarnate in Jesus of Nazareth and was believed by the Sons of Light.

19   The infinite here stands for "endless horizon".

20   The Light is God.

21   To be as God planned me to be *ab Aeterno*.

22   The wedding garment suitable for the wedding of the Lamb (cf. Matt. 22:11-14).

23   Without martyrdom.

24   In other words: what existed in your earthly life.

25   The silence of God that is experienced in creation is ruthless, because it pierces the heart (*transverberation*), posing you an essential

question: who created this marvel?

26 You must understand that you are made for God.

27 One does not speak with the Devil: the weapon to defeat him is silence, fasting and prayer.

28 In Paradise we will be reborn: we will put on Christ (the new MAN).

29 The Son has returned to the Father and has sent the Holy Spirit: the Lily sown in the believers.

30 Quotation in Latin from the Litany of the Blessed Virgin Mary.

31 «It must be known, then, that the soul, after it has been definitively converted to the service of God, is, as a rule, spiritually nurtured and caressed by God, even as is the tender child by its loving mother, who warms it with the heat of her bosom. But, as the child grows bigger, the mother gradually ceases caressing it, and, hiding her tender love, puts bitter aloes upon her sweet breast, sets down the child from her arms and makes it walk upon its feet, so that it may lose the habits of a child and betake itself to more important and substantial occupations.» (John of the Cross, *Dark Night of the Soul*, Newman Press, 1959², p. 18).

32 All of life must be in praise of God; selfishness harms you, the others, the cosmos and God.

33 The Devil speaks badly of you in your mind and before God like an accuser.

34 Providence is seen only with the "eye" of Faith.

35 The Sun here represents God.

36 Which enlightens humanity, that is, the Sons of God.

37 It seems to me that God does not love me.

38 My mind is in difficulty.

39 I need some consolation from a brother in Christ.

40 Without Love (God) there is only boredom.

41 Man in the garden of Eden could eat of all the fruits except that of the knowledge of good and evil. God has imposed this pact.

42 The expulsion of man from the *Garden* is depicted by a *Seraphim* who casts Adam and Eve out of the entrance of the *earthly*

Paradise with a flaming sword.

43   The great sin is Pride: to consider oneself equal to God. What absurdity and foolish arrogance!

44   Man no longer possesses God, who is the Truth.

45   From the living water that springs up to Eternal Life comes Grace, pure as the snow (white is the symbol of purity).

46   Without finding anyone who accepts it.

47   Grace.

48   The Grace generated by God, which dwells in the heart, doe not have its effect, because it is rejected by the human «I».

49   It finds someone who accepts it.

50   Grace or the Light that comes from God.

51   If you put God in the first place in your life, He kisses you and gladdens you.

52   Your heart will then be pure.

53   The soul finds its life (pen).

54   Life is full of Grace.

55   And you live enamored of life!

56   The Holy Spirit: this Presence transforms evil, pain into Good, Joy. This pain in the Communion of the Mystical Body of the Church is a source of Graces for the whole Christian people and the souls of purgatory.

57   With the strength of the Holy Spirit in your heart, you can arrive at being joyful in suffering for the redemption of souls. Thus the present and future, full of pain, can be transfigured in the redeeming and saving Power of the Cross of Jesus Christ.

ACKNOWLEDGEMENTS

I would above all like to thank the Blessed Virgin Mary, the Immaculate, for the unexpected Graces received by the Authors at Lourdes on the level of physical and psychic healing and above all spiritual liberation in May 2016.

Next, special thanks go to the *Associazione Nostra Signora di Lourdes – San Luigi Orione of Missaglia* (Lecco, Italy) and to Pino, with all the Volunteers dedicated to those suffering in the body, the psyche and particularly in the Spirit, in a continuous and successful battle against the prince of darkness, in the Love of Jesus and Mary with the help of the Heavenly Army, guided by the Prince St. Michael the Archangel: *vww.associazionenostrasignoradilourdes.com*.

We cannot forget the Marian Fraternity, at the Marian Sanctuary *Salus Infirmorum* of Scaldaferro (Vicenza, Italy).

We recall with affection Fr. Ireneu Barle, founder and hegumen of the Greco-Catholic Monastery of Prislop (Romania); an intense expression of gratitude goes to the brothers of Opus Dei, and to the Augustinian Nuns already present in the Monastery of Schio and who have now reached the Heavenly Homeland.

Heartfelt thanks go to the nuns of the Servants of Mary of the Monastery of Arco (Trento, Italy) and to the friars Servants of Mary of the convent of Isola Vicentina (Vicenza, Italy).

LITERARY BIOGRAPHY OF THE AUTHOR FRANCESCO SARTORI

Francesco Sartori was born in Schio (Vicenza, Italy) on 13 July 1953. In 1965 he wrote his first poems, and in 1967 won first prize in the Montebello Vicentino national poetry competition.

He attended "Giacomo Zanella" Classical High School in Schio, where he refined his taste for literature. In 1971 he published his first collection of poems *Ho visto Dio* (*I Have Seen God*, New Generation, Rome). In 1972 he obtained his High School Diploma (Classical studies). He then attained a degree in *Religious Sciences* at the Pontifical University of the Holy Cross in Rome, with the maximum score of 90/90 *Summa cum Laude*.

He was editorial coordinator of the series of interreligious ecumenical essays *Figli di Abramo* (*Sons of Abraham*) published by Libreria Editrice Vaticana, for which he also took on the graphic-editorial role, and took third and second place respectively at the 2nd and 3rd «Santa Croce» biennial national prize for religious poetry, organized by the "Santa Croce" ecclesial community of Schio in 1987 and 1989.

A freelance journalist since 1991, the author graduated with 110/110 *cum Laude* in *Audiovisual and Multimedia*

Communication Technology (degree class 16, Communication Sciences) at the Faculty of Arts and Philosophy at the University of Ferrara, where he also attained a Master's in *Digital Technologies and the Net Economy* at the Faculty of Economics and Commerce. Also in Ferrara, he attended the Master's course in *Philosophy* (History of Philosophy). Finally, he attended the Specialist Degree course in *Religious Sciences* at the Pontifical University of the Holy Cross in Rome.

The publishing house Phasar Editions in Florence published the poetic work *Ignudi Naufraghi fra Samo e Patmos* (*Naked Castaways between Samos and Patmos*) in print in October 2003, given an Honourable Mention, along with only five other works, at the 11th Eugenio Montale Prize for European Literature in 2006. The work has received significant reviews in cultural magazines, such as *Il Segnalibro*, and in the national press.

The poetry anthology *Donna di Luce* (*Woman of Light*), also published by Phasar Editions in 2008 and subsequently in 2009 by New Poets Editions in CD format, with reciting voice and original music, won the Special Jury Prize at the City of La Spezia 30th International Competition of Poetry, Fiction and Non-Fiction in 2006.

The poetry anthology *Mistica danza* (*Mystic Dance*), written in collaboration with his son Emanuele, and published by Gondolin Editions of Verona (Fede&Cultura Group) in 2017, was the winner of the published poetry anthology category at the 5th National Prize for Contemporary Italian Literature 2017/2018 promoted by Laura Capone Editor (Rome).

Recently, the relevant international commission included the author, selecting some of his compositions, in World Poetry Day, sponsored by UNESCO and other artistic associations, public bodies and publishing houses.

This event, entitled «*Via Lucis* – poetry as an instrument of light in the search for the absolute and human truths, was held in Venice on 21 March 2018, with the participation of students from Classical High Schools in the Venice region and a poetry reading, curated by university professors and well-known writers.

The author's work also appears in numerous anthologies, including those used in schools, such as *Madre della Tenerezza* (*Mother of Tenderness*, Laura Capone Editor, Rome, 2018). *Madre della Tenerezza* brings together the winning poems, in the unpublished individual poems category, at the 6th National Prize for Contemporary Italian Literature 2018/2019.

His works were awarded the Diploma of Merit by Alessandro Quasimodo, Mogol and Giuseppe Anastasi at the 5th CET Mogol Writers' School Competition in 2018.

Diplomas of Merit were also awarded at the 10th "Il Federiciano" International Poetry Competition in 2018, as well as at the Masterclass of Poetry for Music in 2018, curated by Giuseppe Aletti and Francesco Gazzè.

The author has been selected and participates in the Multimedia Cultural Project «Alessandro Quasimodo Reads the Contemporary Italian Poets», published in 2018, Villanova di Guidonia (Rome), Aletti Editor.

His last book «The Mutations of Love" was the winner in the unpublished poetry anthology category, at the 6th National Prize for Contemporary Italian Literature 2018/2019, promoted by Laura Capone Editor (Rome), and was previewed at the «Book Fair – Open Book» in Florence at the end of September 2018.

This book as translated in French, Spanish and English and was publishing around the world from international Publishing Company, Omniscriptum Publishing Group.

LITERARY BIOGRAPHY OF THE AUTHOR
EMANUELE SARTORI

Emanuele Sartori was born in Schio (Vicenza, Italy) on 20 April 1994 and is the son of the co-author of this work.

He attended the fourth class of High School Technological state with address in Construction, Environment and Territory. His is an inspired composition after a sudden conversion to the Christian faith.

The first of which took place on January 1, 2012, by pure grace given from on high, while was leading a disorderly life and deviated, but still marked by the desire for truth and happiness.

His Poems say the mystical inspiration that pervades it now, after four years of endless tears and suffering caused by the reputation of being abandoned by God. Compositions a month flowed spontaneously, after Emanuele had prayed to God Father of being able to write poems in honor of the B. V. Mary.

These poetry work was the winner of the published poetry anthology category at the 5th National Prize for Contemporary Italian Literature 2017/2018 promoted by Laura Capone Editor (Rome).

The author's works also appears into *Madre della Tenerezza* (*Mother of Tenderness*, Laura Capone Editor, Rome, 2018). *Madre della Tenerezza* brings together the winning poems, in the unpublished individual poems category, at the 6th National Prize for Contemporary Italian Literature 2018/2019.

INDEX

www.ingramcontent.com/pod-product-compliance
Lightning Source LLC
Chambersburg PA
CBHW031846090426
42741CB00005B/377

* 9 7 8 1 9 4 5 6 5 8 1 0 5 *